**INNER ADVENTU**

for # CURIOUS MINDS

MINDFULNESS ACTIVITIES
FOR KIDS 3-5 YEARS OLD
(and their grown-ups)

Curated by Linda Bjork, Founder of Mindfulness Intelligence®

Guided by Lion King Bjork, her fluffy Pomeranian

♥ **INNER ADVENTURES** ♥

for

CURIOUS MINDS

This book belongs to:

_____

Welcome to an Inner Adventure for you and your grown-up! This book is full of fun stories, coloring and puzzle pages, and awesome exercises to strengthen your mindful superpowers: Calm, Focused, and Kind!

Meet Your Inner Adventure Guide:

Lion King the Fluffy Pomeranian

Say hello to Lion King, your friendly guide through this mindfulness adventure!

Lion King isn't just any Pomeranian—he's a fluffy little lion with a big heart and a love for helping kids and grown-ups find their creativity, joy and calm.

Lion King will show you how to breathe like a balloon, stretch like a butterfly, and even listen to the sounds of nature. He believes that every moment can be an adventure when you're curious and mindful.

Ready to join him?

Let's go on a mindful adventure together!

Dear Grown-Ups,

Welcome to Inner Adventures!

This activity book is designed to help you and your little one slow down, connect, and explore mindfulness together.

Through playful activities, calming exercises, and engaging stories, you'll experience how small moments of presence can make a big difference in your child's resilience, growth, and well-being.

As you journey through these pages with Lion King as your guide, you'll discover simple ways to encourage curiosity, creativity, and calm.

Whether it's stretching like a lion, sharing a mindful story, or exploring through coloring, these moments are more than fun—they're tools for building focus, kindness, and emotional regulation.

Let's begin this adventure together!

How to Use This Book

This book is a treasure trove of mindful activities for you and your child to explore at your own pace. Here are a few tips to get the most out of it:

The book has three sections, each with distinct themes, including a short story, mindful movement, coloring, puzzles, and other mindful activities.

 IN THE MINDFUL WOODS

 IN MINDFUL SPACE

 ON A MINDFUL FARM

Keep in Mind:

Storytime fosters connection! Each story is followed by a coloring spread that encourages grown-ups and kids to work together.

Join the fun! Whether you're coloring together or practicing a stretch, your participation enriches the experience.

Kids enjoy repetition! Returning to familiar activities helps build comfort and confidence.

Celebrate Small Wins! Mindfulness is a journey, not a race, so celebrate every moment of connection and calm that you share.

Materials Checklist

Here's what you might want to have handy for your inner adventures:

Crayons or Markers for creative coloring fun

Favorite Teddy for exercises or cuddles

Pillows for mindful sitting and extra cozyness

Blanket or Yoga Mat for mindful movement

Quiet Space free from distractions

Open Minds and Hearts, ready for connection and fun!

Table of Contents

All three activity chapters are filled with fun and engaging coloring and puzzle pages. Each short story is accompanied by a coloring spread where kids and grown-ups can reflect and color together.

Mindfulness Benefits for Kids 11

A Short Mindful Story: *The Slow, Brave Snail* 13

ACTIVITY CHAPTERS:

   1. IN THE MINDFUL WOODS
     Short Story: *The Gentle Wind* 19

   2. IN MINDFUL SPACE
     Short Story: *The Cosmic Calm* 45

   3. ON A MINDFUL FARM
     Short Story: *Lion King Helps Out* 71

SLEEPING WELL WITH MINDFULNESS
Short Story: *The Moonbeam* 97

MINDFUL MOVEMENT:
Poses for 3-5 year-olds (and their parents)
Instructions for grown-ups 105

Answer Keys 111

Elements of Connection and Co-Creation

Independent Work: This book includes pages designed for independent activities for children aged 3 to 5.

Collaborative Connection: Every page and exercise encourages collaboration between you and your child.

Co-Creative Coloring: After each short story, utilize the collaborative coloring spread.

Mindful Movements: Whether you follow the mindful movements in each activity chapter or complete a whole set from the resource pages, take the chance to engage in these mindful exercises with your child.

Create a Routine: Establishing a cozy "mindfulness corner" at home can help transform mindfulness into a comforting habit.

Bedtime Success: Incorporate reflection, gratitude, and calming exercises to foster healthy sleep habits.

BETTER SLEEP   MORE CONFIDENCE   MORE KINDNESS

Mindfulness Benefits for Kids

Mindfulness is like a magical superpower that helps kids grow happy, healthy, and strong. Here's what it can do:

Focus, even amid distractions: Mindfulness enables kids to pay attention and stay on task.

Stay calm, even under pressure: Mindful breathing and movement can help reduce big feelings like frustration or worry.

Choose kindness, even in adversity: Children learn to show kindness to themselves and others by practicing gratitude and compassion.

Feel safe and strong: Mindfulness builds confidence and resilience, helping kids handle changes and challenges.

With practice, these skills will develop, just as a small seed transforms into a big, beautiful tree.

BETTER FOCUS LESS STRESS MORE RESILIENCE

Dear Grown-Ups,

Reading with your child is a great way to nurture their growing mind and heart while building a sense of security and love—these moments of connection plant seeds of curiosity, creativity, and resilience.

The short, mindful stories with Lion King invite calmness, awareness, and self-discovery, offering a chance to slow down and connect.

The coloring pages accompanying each story encourage meaningful conversations and deeper engagement between awesome grown-ups and adventurous kids.

Enjoy this mindful journey together!

A SHORT MINDFUL STORY

Lion King introduces the first mindful story and coloring spread in your activity book!

The Slow, Brave Snail

Lion King was racing through the garden when he saw a little snail inching along a leaf. "Why are you so slow, snail?" Lion King asked.

The snail smiled, "Because I like to notice everything on the way!" Curious, Lion King sat down and looked closer. He saw tiny raindrops sparkling like diamonds, a ladybug resting on a flower, and even the warm sunlight dancing on the grass.

"Wow," said Lion King, "I miss so much when I go too fast!" From then on, Lion King remembered to slow down and enjoy the little things, just like the snail.

It's okay to take your time and enjoy the little things in life.

AWESOME GROWN-UP SIDE

ADVENTUROUS KID SIDE

IN THE MINDFUL WOODS

ACTIVITY CHAPTER 1

The Gentle Wind

Lion King was playing in the forest when a gentle wind began to blow. The leaves danced, the flowers swayed, and the tall trees whispered soft secrets.

"What are they saying?" Lion King wondered. He stopped running and sat still, letting the wind tickle his fur.

As he listened, he noticed the buzzing bees, the chirping birds, and even the sound of his own breath. "The forest is so alive!" he thought, feeling calm and happy.

From that day, Lion King made time to pause and listen to the forest's music.

Take a moment to pause and notice the world around you.

AWESOME GROWN-UP SIDE

ADVENTUROUS KID SIDE

Tree Pose

Balance on one leg, raise the other leg's foot to the ankle or knee of the supporting leg. Put the palms together in front of the chest and raise them up above the head. Balance and breathe!

Next, switch legs.

One mindfulness yoga pose is called the tree pose!
Can you pretend to be a tree?

Hugs and smiles make us feel safe and loved. That's probably why we love our stuffies and teddies so much!

Coloring time!

The bear loves his teddy bear.

What's your favorite stuffie?

Holding a smooth rock or feeling soft fabric can help us calm our minds and bodies, turning nervous energy into a sense of comfort and focus.

The Calm Pebble

When Lion King feels nervous or scared, he holds a small rock that he calls "my calm pebble."

To get your own calm pebble, paint and decorate a rock—or draw one below!

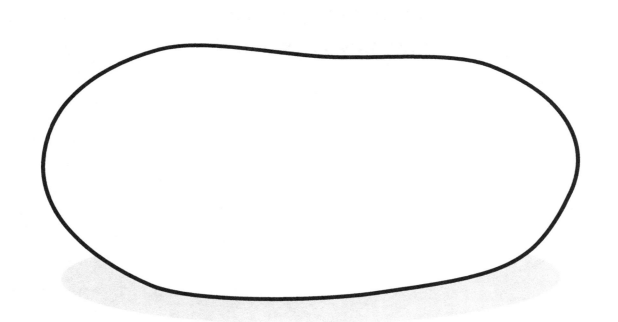

The forest seems quiet.
But when we listen
closely, we hear rustling
leaves, chirping birds,
and maybe even a fox!

Where does Fox live?
Fox needs some color magic!

What we eat should
taste good and make us
feel good!

Does Bunny want an acorn or a carrot?

What's your favorite snack?

If you can't find a toy, try to close your eyes and see if your memory can remind you where it is.

Can you help Squirrel find her acorn?
Tell Squirrel which path to take!

1

2

3

X

X

Have you ever eaten fruits or berries that you have just picked from a vine or tree?

What colors do apples come in? Color three different ones and then color the apple barrel!

Listening to birds chirping is a relaxing and fun thing to do. Chirping is how birds speak!

Someone built a birdhouse in the woods!
Can you put some color on it?

We don't have to smile
when we're sad or angry.
But when we feel ready,
it's a great idea to smile,
because it makes us feel
better. Try it!

Outdoor Smiles

Can you think of four things that make you smile outdoors?

Maybe clouds or birds?

Or flowers or rocks?

Or swings or meeting dogs?

Draw them below!

THIS MAKES ME SMILE:

THAT MAKES ME SMILE:

THIS TOO:

AND THAT:

Deer have great hearing,
which helps them stay
alert, and hedgehogs roll
into a ball to feel safe.
Maybe you curl up and
listen sometimes, too?

Deer and Hedgehog are dear friends!
Let's put some color to them!

IN MINDFUL SPACE

ACTIVITY CHAPTER 2

The Cosmic Calm

Lion King was floating in space, visiting the sparkling stars and zooming comets. Suddenly, a giant asteroid zoomed by, and Lion King's spaceship started to wobble.

"Oh no, what do I do?" he thought, his little paws trembling.

Then, he remembered Wise Owl's advice: "Take a deep breath in, little lion, and your calm will guide you."

Lion King closed his eyes, breathed in deeply, and let out a big, slow sigh. The spaceship steadied, and Lion King felt ready to face any adventure.

"Even in space, calm is my superpower!" he said, floating toward the stars.

When you feel overwhelmed, breathe slowly and find your calm.

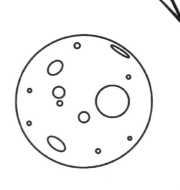

AWESOME GROWN-UP SIDE

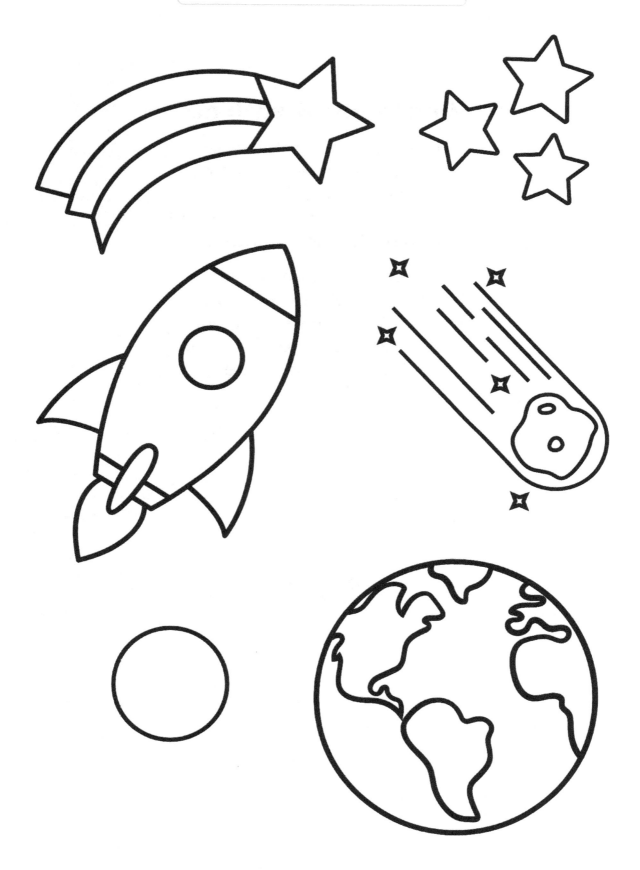

ADVENTUROUS KID SIDE

Mindfulness Breathing

Sit down in a comfortable position or lie down on a mat. Close your eyes. Turn your attention to your inner space and listen to the silence within.

The calm rhythm of your breathing feels soothing and restful. You might even want to cover your ears to hear your breath from the inside!

With mindfulness, you can travel to the silence of space within you. Try it yourself!

Rockets reach zero gravity
(the feeling of weightlessness)
just 8-10 minutes after launch.
That's how fast they zoom
into space!

Coloring time!

This rocket needs some color to lift off!

The first living being to orbit earth was a stray dog named Laika. Because of Laika, it was easier to later send humans into space.

Lion King has picked letters for you to fill in with color! Can you read the words they make? Can you write the words on the line under the letters?

Write here: _

Write here: _

In space, there's no air to breathe or carry sound, so it's completely silent. That's why astronauts wear special suits with air tanks!

Our friend is having fun in space.
Can you draw a face and color the
space suit?

You have a big, calm space within you where your mind can drift and feel relaxed and weightless. Just like an astronaut!

Can you help the astronaut find the spaceship?

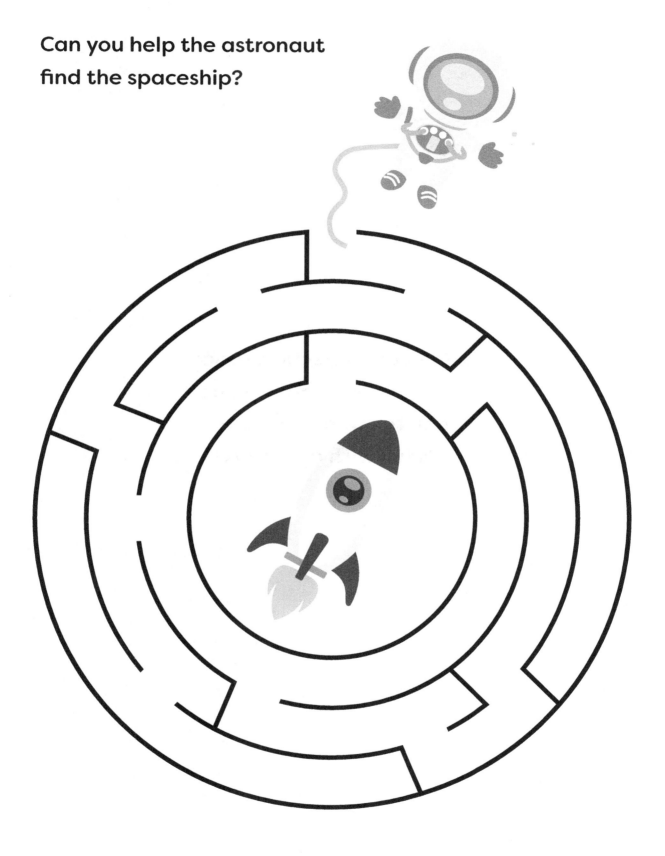

U.F.O.s are objects in space
that not even grown-ups
can tell what they are.
It's fun with a mystery!

Wait a minute! Is that a CAT floating around in SPACE? Perhaps the cat wants to say hi to the U.F.O?

Our galaxy, the Milky Way, has about 100 billion stars. When we think about how space is infinite (that there is no end), we can feel in awe.

Can you color and count the stars?

Can you color and count the planets?

Items on a spaceship
are weightless when the
spaceship is orbiting Earth.
If they're not fastened, they
float around!

Uh-oh! Astronaut's snacks are floating around in the spaceship! Catch and color them!

When we find the right words to describe our feelings, we can better understand what we need to feel better. We also understand our friends better!

Our feelings show up on our faces! Can you draw eyes, eyebrows, and mouth on each face for the feelings below?

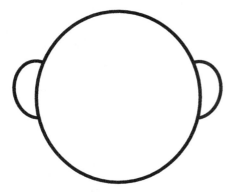

Glad/Happy

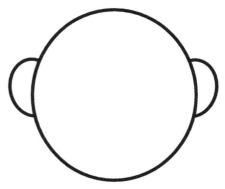

Shocked/Surprised

Neutral/Satisfied

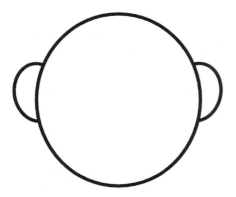

Angry/Frustrated

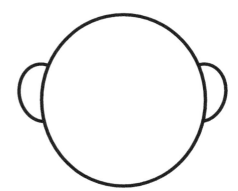

Sad/Down

In mindfulness, we learn to
focus and pay attention.

Can you spot three differences between the picture on the right and the picture on the left?

_____

_____

_____

ON A MINDFUL FARM

ACTIVITY CHAPTER 3

Lion King Helps Out

One sunny morning, Lion King grabbed his little shovel and bucket and trotted off to the barn. Farmer Jill smiled, "Good morning, Lion King! The cows are waiting for their breakfast—want to help?" Lion King's eyes lit up. "Yes, please!" he said, wagging his fluffy tail.

Farmer Jill showed him how to scoop the grain into his bucket. As he poured the grain in, the cows trotted over, mooing happily. "They look so excited!" Lion King giggled. He noticed how strong his paws felt as he carried the bucket and how good it felt to help.

When the cows finished eating, one gave a soft "moo" that sounded like "thank you." Lion King beamed. "Helping out isn't just fun—it makes everyone, even me, feel happy!" he said, brushing some hay off his fur. Farmer Jill nodded, "That's the magic of lending a paw, Lion King."

Helping others can make us feel happy and connected.

AWESOME GROWN-UP SIDE

ADVENTUROUS KID SIDE

Mountain Pose

Stand tall with your feet hip-width apart and arms relaxed by your sides. Press your feet into the ground and imagine growing as tall as a strong mountain as you lift your hands to reach the top of your head.

Take a deep, calming breath. Feel steady and strong.

In mindfulness yoga, we get to be big, strong mountains! Now, it's your turn.

Chickens can count up
to five and recognize
more than 100 faces,
including humans!

Chicken is riding on the roof of the tractor.

What does Chicken see from there?

Let's color this page!

The largest pumpkin ever grown weighed over 2,700 pounds—that's about as heavy as a small car!

How silly! A huge pumpkin is on a small car!
What colors do you want to make them?

When we eat our snacks
mindfully, we taste each
yummy bite and enjoy
every moment.

Cow tells Lion King that a snack would be great.
Which snack is available? Trace Cow's track to the snack!

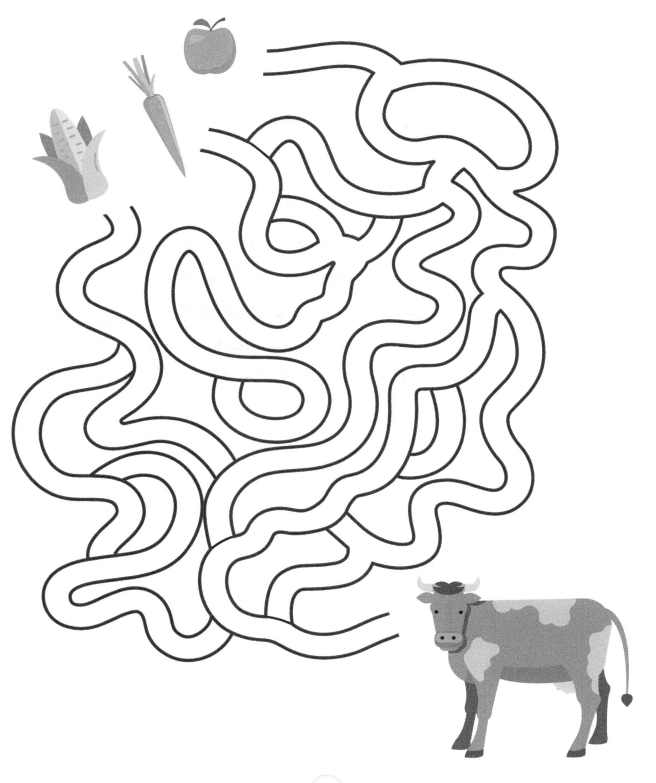

There are over 7,500 types of apples in the world! If you tried a new apple every day, it would take more than 20 years to taste them all.

The farmer has filled the farm stand.

Can you color it to make it look delicious?

Pigs are as smart as a 3-year-old child! They can learn their names, play games, and even solve puzzles.

What do you want to name Pig?

Can you help _____

get to their puzzle book?

PIG PUZZLES

Ears hear amazing things! Elephants can hear storms from far away. Dogs and cats hear sounds that humans can't hear. Rabbits have large, movable ears that can rotate one at a time!

Listening Ears Game

Our friend Bunny has big ears. Join Bunny's favorite listening game!

Listen closely to nearby sounds. What do you hear? What do sounds look like?

Draw them below!

Benny says that sometimes it's easier to hear if you close your eyes.

HOW I SEE A SOUND I HEAR NOW:

DRAWING ANOTHER SOUND I HEAR NOW:

MY DRAWING OF A FIRE ENGINE'S SOUND:

HOW I SEE THE SOUND OF BIRDS CHIRPING:

Sometimes, feeling really mad is called 'seeing red.' But red is also known as the color of love! What does red mean to you?

Can all these different things be red? Let's color and see!

Cats purr when they feel
good and calm or to make
themselves feel better!
What makes you feel calm?

Tracing Ms Kitty

Can you trace the lines for Ms Kitty before you color her on her comfy chair?

Happy feelings are good
for you—they help you
fight off bad germs!

Baby farm animals are so cute!
Baby Cow, Baby Alpaca, and Baby
Pig need some color!

Dear Grown-ups,

Bedtime isn't just the end of the day—it's a special moment to connect, comfort, and prepare for a restful night.

Creating a mindful bedtime routine helps your child feel secure and loved. It also gives their growing bodies and busy minds a chance to recharge. Consistent bedtime habits support healthy sleep patterns, boost learning, and strengthen your child's immune system.

This section presents a simple mindfulness activity, the breathing buddy, along with a soothing nighttime story featuring Lion King to create a peaceful, shared experience at bedtime.

These practices will not only help your child fall asleep more easily but also cultivate a sense of connection and relaxation for both of you. Think of bedtime as a gift—a chance to pause, snuggle, and reflect on the good things to round off the day.

Sweet dreams await!

SLEEPING WELL

With Mindfulness

Belly Buddy Breathing

Get your favorite soft teddy, lie down, put the teddy on your belly, and watch the teddy slowly move up and down to the rhythm of your breathing.

If you have more than one favorite teddy, you can let them take turns!

Breathing with your belly buddy is a great way to calm down and prepare for sleepy time! Let your grown-up read a calming story as you drift off to sleep.

The Friendly Moonbeam

At bedtime, Lion King looked out the window and saw a bright moonbeam shining into his room. "What are you doing here, moonbeam?" he asked.

The moonbeam giggled, "I'm here to remind you of all the good things that happened today!"

Lion King thought about playing tag with his friends, the yummy snack his mom made, and the story his dad read to him.

"Thank you, moonbeam," he said, snuggling under his blanket. "I feel happy just thinking about those things." The moonbeam smiled and softly whispered, "That's the magic of gratitude, little lion."

Gratitude helps us feel happy and peaceful.

AWESOME GROWN-UP SIDE

ADVENTUROUS KID SIDE

Dear Grown-ups,

Mindful movement exercises provide a wonderful way to slow down, breathe deeply, and share moments of presence that nurture both the body and mind.

These simple yet powerful practices assist kids in developing balance, focus, and coordination while modeling healthy habits they can carry throughout their lives.

As parents and guardians, you can help your children discover how joyful and calming movement can be. Whether stretching like a butterfly, standing tall like a mountain, or becoming a brave little warrior, these exercises encourage creativity, self-awareness, and bonding.

By practicing together, you're not only moving and creating memories of connection but also teaching the importance of a strong, mindful foundation. Make this a playful and purposeful habit.

MINDFUL MOVEMENT

Instructions

Mindful Movement

Kids and grown-ups! Let's use our bodies for some mindful movement together! In the activity chapters, we've been introduced to three different mindful poses: the tree pose, mindful breathing, and the mountain pose.

Here they are all in one place!

Tree Pose

Balance on one leg, raise the other leg's foot to the ankle of the supporting leg. Put the palms together in front of the chest and raise them up above the head. Balance and breathe! Next, switch legs.

Mindfulness Breathing

Sit down in a comfortable position or lie down on a mat. Close your eyes. Turn your attention to your inner space and listen to the silence within.

The calm rhythm of your breathing feels soothing and restful. You might even want to cover your ears to hear your breath from the inside!

Mindful Movement

Mindful movement is not a competition but a way to connect with our bodies, minds, and each other!

Engage in mindful movement for a few minutes each day to enjoy greater focus, calm, and improved body awareness.

GREAT NEWS!

Further instructions for grown-ups on the next page!

BREATHE EASY!

Mountain Pose

Stand tall with your feet hip-width apart and arms relaxed by your sides. Press your feet into the ground and imagine growing as tall as a strong mountain as you lift your hands to reach the top of your head. Take a deep, calming breath. Feel steady and strong.

Mindful Movement

Grown-ups!

Here are more detailed instructions on how to lead your little one in mindful movements. Choose a quiet and comfy place and join the mindful fun!

Tree Pose

Instructions

- Join your child and stand tall with your feet together and arms by your sides. Say, "Let's be trees! Start as a trunk standing still."

- Lift one foot and rest it on your ankle or calf (but not on the knee). Stretch your arms out to the sides or reach them up high, like tree branches.

- Encourage a little wobble, saying, "If the wind makes your tree sway, that's okay—trees are flexible!"

- After a few breaths, gently lower your foot and switch sides to grow your tree on the other side. "Look at your tall, beautiful tree!"

In mindfulness, we respect everyone's comfort level.

Mindfulness Breathing
Instructions

- Cross your legs like a butterfly or sit on a soft cushion and ask your child to do the same.

- If your child feels comfortable, ask them to close their eyes or place a teddy in front of them on which they can fixate their gaze.

- For the inhale, we breathe like a balloon: Ask your child to take a big breath in through their nose, pretending their belly is a balloon.

- For the exhale, we blow out like a candle: Ask them to blow out slowly and gently through their mouth, like blowing out a birthday candle, but slower.

- Repeat: Practice 5-10 breaths, encouraging them to feel how calm their body gets. Say, "You're making your body feel calm and strong!"

- End with a smile and ask, "How do you feel now?" Ending the calm practice with a big hug is recommended!

Mountain Pose
Instructions

- Ask your child to stand up tall with their feet together and arms resting at their sides. Say, "Be as tall and still as a mountain!"

- Reach for the Sky: Encourage them to stretch their arms up high, like the peak of a mountain touching the clouds.

- Feel Strong and Grounded: Prompt them to press their feet into the ground, like the roots of a mountain reaching deep into the Earth.

- Take a Big Breath: "Inhale and feel the wind around your mountain, then exhale gently!" Conclude by saying, "You're strong, steady, and calm, just like a mountain!"

You are amazing,
just as you are.

Answer Keys

Figuring things out is fun! If you are curious about answers to some of the puzzles, here they are!

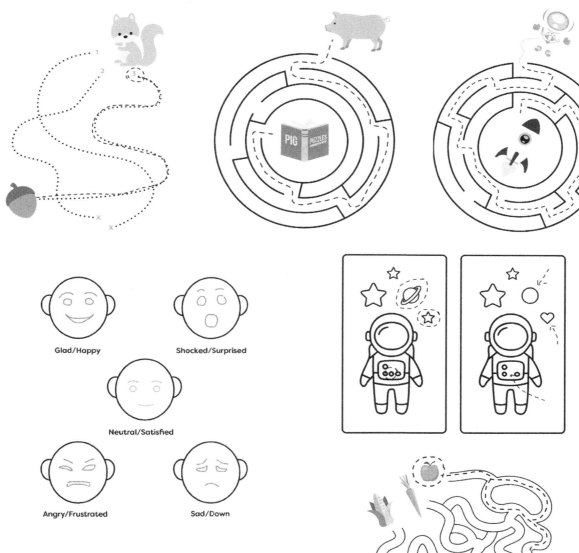

Glad/Happy

Shocked/Surprised

Neutral/Satisfied

Angry/Frustrated

Sad/Down

Remember, mindful activities is not about doing it right, but being present and enjoying the moment.

See you soon!

Let's Play More!

Lion King would love to do more mindful coloring and puzzles with you! The Inner Adventures series have more mindful activitity books—for kids, teenagers, and adults! Make sure to check back for more at the resources below.

WEB:

lindabjork.org/inneradventures

INSTAGRAM:

@inner_adventures_series

AMAZON:

amazon.com/author/bjork

Cover design by Bjork Business. The fonts in this book are licensed and created with Adobe Creative Suite. The graphics are created using Adobe Creative Suite, Canva, and D-zine.

ISBN: 979-8-9915287-2-6 (paperback)

Book Title:
Curious Minds: Mindfulness Activities for Kids 3-5 Years Old (and their parents) from the Inner Adventures Series

Linda Bjork, February 2025